BESTSELLING CHRISTIAN BOOKS

- 51 Most Powerful Prayers by Ryan
  Christianity/Prayers, ISBN: 9789354990847
- A Christmas Carol by Charles Dickens
  Christianity, ISBN: 9788193545874
- A Cloud by Day, a Fire by Night by AW Tozer
  Christianity/Inspiration, ISBN: 9789354990854
- Absolute Surrender by Andrew Murray
  Christianity, ISBN: 9789389716269
- Awakened Imagination by Neville Goddard
  Christianity, ISBN: 9789389157086
- Be What You Wish by Neville Goddard
  Christianity, ISBN: 9789387669550
- Delighting in God by AW Tozer
  Christianity/Good & Evil, ISBN: 9788194748632
- Experiencing the Holy Spirit by Andrew Murray
  Christianity, ISBN: 9788194764809
- Feeling is the Secret by Neville Goddard
  Christianity, ISBN: 9789389157109
- How to be Filled with the Holy Spirit by AW Tozer
  Christianity, ISBN: 9789389157116
- In His Steps by Charles M. Sheldon
  Christianity, ISBN: 9789390492794
- Life of Christ by Fulton J. Sheen
  Christianity/New Testament, ISBN: 9789389716306

Search the book by its ISBN

PRAYER

The Art of Believing

NEVILLE GODDARD

GENERAL PRESS

Published by

GENERAL PRESS

4805/24, Fourth Floor, Krishna House
Ansari Road, Daryaganj, New Delhi - 110002
Ph : 011-23282971, 45795759
E-mail : generalpressindia@gmail.com

www.generalpress.in

First Edition : 2023

ISBN : 9789354994487

Published by Azeem Ahmad Khan for General Press

Contents

About the Author

Neville Lancelot Goddard was born on February 19, 1905 on the then British-protectorate of Barbados in the town of St. Michael to an Anglican family of nine sons and one daughter. A 1950s gossip column described the young Neville as "enormously wealthy," his family possessing "a whole island in the West Indies."

The truth was far more modest. Neville depicted his own English childhood home as happy, but threadbare. There was constant jostling among his brothers for clothes and second-helpings at the dinner table. Neville came to New York City at the age of seventeen to study theater – a move that led to a successful career as a vaudeville dancer and Broadway actor. He toured America and England with dance troupes. But Neville's theater life was hand-to-mouth; he supplemented his income by working as an elevator operator and shipping clerk.

The young performer's ambition for the stage began to fade as he encountered an alluring range of spiritual ideas – first with self-styled occult groups, and later with the help of a life-transforming mentor. In his lectures, Neville described studying with a turbaned, Ethiopian-born rabbi named Abdullah. Their initial meeting, Neville said, had an air of kismet:

When I first met my friend Abdullah back in 1931 I entered a room where he was speaking and when the speech was ended he came over, extended his hand and said: "Neville, you are six months late." I had never seen the man before, so I said: "I am six months late? How do you know me?" and he replied: "The brothers told me that you were coming and you are six months late."

According to Neville, the two studied Hebrew, Scripture, and Kabbalah together for five years – planting the seeds of Neville's philosophy of mental creativity.

Neville said that his first understanding of the power of creative thought came while he was living in a rented room on Manhattan's Upper West Side during the winter of 1933. The young man was depressed: his theatrical career had stalled and his pockets were empty. "After twelve years in America, I was a failure in my own eyes," he later said. "I was in the theater and made money one year and spent it the next month." The 28-year-old ached to spend Christmas with his family in Barbados; but he couldn't afford to travel.

"Live as though you are there," Abdullah told him, "and that you shall be." Wandering the streets of New York City, Neville thought from his aim – as he would later urge his listeners – and adopted the feeling that he was really and truly at home on his native island. "Abdullah taught me the importance of remaining faithful to an idea and not compromising," he recalled. "I wavered, but he remained faithful to the assumption that I was in Barbados and had traveled first class."

One December morning before the last ship was to depart New York that year for Barbados, Neville received a letter from a long out-of-touch brother: In it was $50 and a ticket to sail. His experiment, it seemed, had worked.

Neville discovered what eventually became the hallmark of his philosophy: It is imperative to assume the feeling that one's goal has already been attained. "It is not what you want that you attract," he wrote. "You attract what you believe to be true."

Prayer is the master key. A key may fit one door of a house, but when it fits all doors it may well claim to be a master key. Such and no less a key is prayer to all earthly problems.

CHAPTER 1

Law of Reversibility

"Pray for my soul, more things are wrought by prayer than this world dreams of" (Tennyson).

Prayer is an art and requires practice. The first requirement is a controlled imagination. Parade and vain repetitions are foreign to prayer. Its exercise requires tranquility and peace of mind, "Use not vain repetitions," for prayer is done in secret and "thy Father which seeth in secret shall reward thee openly." The ceremonies that are customarily used in prayer are mere superstitions and have been invented to give prayer an air of solemnity. Those who do practice the art of prayer are often ignorant of the laws that control it. They attribute the results obtained to the ceremonies and mistake the letter for the spirit. The essence of prayer is faith; but faith must be permeated with understanding to be given that active quality which it does not possess when standing alone. "Therefore, get wisdom; and with all thy getting get understanding."

This book is an attempt to reduce the unknown to the known, by pointing out conditions on which prayers are answered, and without which they cannot be answered. It defines the conditions governing prayer in laws that are simply a generalization of our observations.

The universal law of reversibility is the foundation on which its claims are based.

Mechanical motion caused by speech was known for a long time before anyone dreamed of the possibility of an inverse transformation, that is, the reproduction of speech by mechanical motion (the phonograph). For a long time electricity was produced by friction without ever a thought that friction, in turn, could be produced by electricity. Whether or not man succeeds in reversing the transformation of a force, he knows, nevertheless, that all transformations of force *are* reversible. If heat can produce mechanical motion, so mechanical motion can produce heat. If electricity produces magnetism, magnetism too can develop electric currents. If the voice can cause undulatory currents, so can such currents reproduce the voice, and so on. Cause and effect, energy and matter, action and reaction are the same and inter-convertible.

This law is of the highest importance, because it enables you to foresee the inverse transformation once the direct transformation is verified. If you knew how you would *feel* were you to realize your objective, then, inversely, you would know what state you could realize were you to awaken in yourself such feeling. The injunction, to pray believing that you already possess what you pray for, is based upon a knowledge of the law of inverse transformation. If your realized prayer produces in you a definite feeling or state of consciousness, then, inversely, that particular feeling or state of consciousness *must* produce your realized prayer. Because all transformations of force are reversible, you should always assume the feeling of your fulfilled wish.

You should awaken within you the *feeling* that you are and have that which heretofore you desired to be and possess. This is easily done by contemplating the joy that would be yours were your objective an accomplished fact, so that you live and move and have your being in the feeling that your wish is realized.

The feeling of the wish fulfilled, if assumed and sustained, must objectify the state that would have created it. This law explains why "Faith is the substance of things hoped for, the evidence of things not seen" and why "He calleth things that are not seen *as though they were* and things that were not seen become seen." Assume the feeling of your wish fulfilled and continue feeling that it is fulfilled until that which you feel objectifies itself.

If a physical fact can produce a psychological state, a psychological state can produce a physical fact. If the effect (a) can be produced by the cause (b), then inversely, the effect (b) can be produced by the cause (a). Therefore I say unto you, "What things soever ye desire, when ye pray, believe that ye have received them, and ye shall have them" (Mark 11:24).

CHAPTER 2

Dual Nature of Consciousness

A clear concept of the dual nature of man's consciousness must be the basis of all true prayer. Consciousness includes a subconscious as well as a conscious part. The infinitely greater part of consciousness lies below the sphere of objective consciousness. The subconscious is the most important part of consciousness. It is the cause of voluntary action. The subconscious is what a man *is*. The conscious is what a man *knows*. "I and my Father are one but my Father is greater than I." The conscious and subconscious are one, but the subconscious is greater than the conscious.

"I of myself can do nothing, the Father within me He doeth the work." I, objective consciousness, of myself can do nothing; the Father, the subconscious, He doeth the work. The subconscious is that in which everything is known, in which everything is possible, to which everything goes, from which everything comes, which belongs to all, to which all have access.

What we are conscious of is constructed out of what we are not conscious of. Not only do our subconscious assumptions influence our behavior but they also fashion the pattern of our objective existence. They alone have the power to say, "Let us make man—objective manifestations—in our image, after our likeness." The whole of creation is asleep within the deep of man and is awakened to objective existence by his subconscious assumptions. Within that blankness we call sleep there is a consciousness in unsleeping vigilance, and while the body sleeps this unsleeping being releases from the treasure house of eternity the subconscious assumptions of man.

Prayer is the key which unlocks the infinite storehouse. "Prove me now herewith, saith the Lord of hosts, if I will not open you the windows of heaven, and pour you out a blessing, that there shall not be room enough to receive it." Prayer modifies or completely changes our subconscious assumptions, and a change of assumption is a change of expression.

The conscious mind reasons inductively from observation, experience and education. It therefore finds it difficult to believe what the five senses and inductive reason deny. The subconscious reasons deductively and is never concerned with the truth or falsity of the premise but proceeds on the assumption of the correctness of the premise and objectifies results which are consistent with the premise. This distinction must be clearly seen by all who would master the art of praying. No true grasp of the science of prayer can be really obtained until the laws governing the dual nature of consciousness are understood and the importance of the subconscious realized.

Prayer—the art of believing what is denied by the senses—deals almost entirely with the subconscious. Through prayer, the subconscious is suggested into acceptance of the wish fulfilled, and, reasoning deductively, logically unfolds it to its legitimate end. "Far greater is He that is in you than he that is in the world."

The subjective mind is the diffused consciousness that animates the world; it is the spirit that giveth life. In all substance is a single soul—subjective mind. Through all creation runs this one unbroken subjective mind. Thought and feeling fused into beliefs impress modifications upon it, charge it with a mission, which mission it faithfully executes.

The conscious mind originates premises. The subjective mind unfolds them to their logical ends. Were the subjective mind not so limited in its initiative power of reasoning, objective man could not be held responsible for his actions in the world. Man transmits ideas to the subconscious through his feelings. The subconscious transmits ideas from mind to mind through telepathy. Your unexpressed convictions of others are transmitted to them without their conscious knowledge or consent, and if subconsciously accepted by them will influence their behavior.

The only ideas they subconsciously reject are your ideas of them which they could not wish to be true of anyone. Whatever they could wish for others can be believed of them, and by the law of belief which governs subjective reasoning they are compelled to subjectively accept, and therefore objectively express, accordingly.

The subjective mind is completely controlled by suggestion. Ideas are best suggested when the objective mind is partly subjective, that is, when the objective senses are diminished or held in abeyance. This partly subjective state can best be described as *controlled reverie*, wherein the mind is passive but capable of functioning with absorption. It is a concentration of attention.

There must be no conflict in your mind when you are praying. Turn from what *is* to what *ought to be*. Assume the mood of fulfilled desire, and by the universal law of reversibility you will realize your desire.

CHAPTER 3

Imagination and Faith

Prayers are not successfully made unless there is a rapport between the conscious and subconscious mind of the operator. This is done through imagination and faith.

By the power of imagination all men, certainly imaginative men, are forever casting forth enchantments, and all men, especially unimaginative men, are continually passing under their power. Can we ever be certain that it was not our mother while darning our socks who began that subtle change in our minds? If I can unintentionally cast an enchantment over persons, there is no reason to doubt that I am able to cast intentionally a far stronger enchantment.

Everything, that can be seen, touched, explained, argued over, is to the imaginative man nothing more than a means, for he functions, by reason of his controlled imagination, in the deep of him-self where every idea exists in itself and not in relation to something else. In him there is no need for the restraints of reason. For the only restraint he can obey is the mysterious instinct that teaches him to eliminate all moods other than the mood of the fulfilled desire.

Imagination and faith are the only faculties of the mind needed to create objective conditions. The faith required for the successful operation of the law of consciousness is a purely subjective faith and is attainable upon the cessation of active opposition on the part of the objective mind of the operator. It depends on your ability to feel and accept as true what your objective senses deny. Neither the passivity of the subject nor his conscious agreement with your suggestion is necessary, for without his consent or knowledge he can be given a subjective order which he must objectively express. It is a fundamental law of consciousness that by telepathy we can have immediate communion with another.

To establish rapport you call the subject mentally. Focus your attention on him and mentally shout his name just as you would to attract the attention of anyone. Imagine that he answered, and mentally hear his voice. Represent him to yourself inwardly in the state you want him to obtain. Then imagine that he is telling you in the tones of ordinary conversation what you want to hear. Mentally answer him. Tell him of your joy in witnessing his good fortune. Having mentally heard with all the distinctness of reality that which you wanted to hear and having thrilled to the news heard, return to objective consciousness. Your subjective conversation must awaken what it affirmed.

"Thou shalt decree a thing and it shall be established unto thee." It is not a strong will that sends the subjective word on its mission so much as it is clear thinking and feeling the truth of the state affirmed. When belief and will are in conflict, belief invariably wins. "Not by might, nor by power, but by my spirit, saith the Lord of hosts."

It is not what you want that you attract; you attract what you believe to be true. Therefore, get into the spirit of these mental conversations and give them the same degree of reality that you would a telephone conversation. "If thou canst believe, all things are possible to him that believeth. Therefore, I say unto you, what things soever you desire, when you pray, believe that ye received them, and ye shall have them." The acceptance of the end wills the means. And the wisest reflection could not devise more effective means than those which are willed by the acceptance of the end. Mentally talk to your friends as though your desires for them were already realized.

Imagination is the beginning of the growth of all forms, and faith is the substance out of which they are formed. By imagination, that which exists in latency or is asleep within the deep of consciousness is awakened and is given form. The cures attributed to the influence of certain medicines, relics and places are the effects of imagination and faith. The curative power is not in the spirit that is in them, it is in the spirit in which they are accepted. "The letter killeth, but the spirit giveth life."

The subjective mind is completely controlled by suggestion, so, whether the object of your faith be true or false, you will get the same results. There is nothing unsound in the theory of medicine or in the claims of priesthood for their relics and holy places. The subjective mind of the patient accepts the suggestion of health conditioned on such states, and as soon as these conditions are met proceeds to realize health. "According to your faith be it done unto you for all things are possible to him that believeth." Confident expectation of a state is the most potent means of bringing it about. The confident expectation of a cure does that which no medical treatment can accomplish.

Failure is always due to an antagonistic auto-suggestion by the patient, arising from objective doubt of the power of medicine or relic, or from doubt of the truth of the theory. Many of us, either from too little emotion or too much intellect, both of which are stumbling blocks in the way or prayer, cannot believe that which our sense deny. To force ourselves to believe will end in greater doubt. To avoid such counter-suggestions the patient should be unaware, objectively, of the suggestions which are made to him. The most effective method of healing or influencing the behavior of others consists in what is known as "the silent or absent treatment." When the subject is unaware, objectively, of the suggestion given him there is no possibility of him setting up an antagonistic belief. It is not necessary that the patient know, objectively, that anything is being done for him. From what is known of the subjective and objective processes of reasoning, it is better that he should not know objectively of that which is being done for him. The more completely the objective mind is kept in ignorance of the suggestion, the better will the subjective mind perform its functions. The subject subconsciously accepts the suggestion and thinks he originates it, proving the truth of Spinoza's dictum that we know not the causes that determine our actions.

The subconscious mind is the universal conductor which the operator modifies with his thoughts and feelings. Visible states are either the vibratory effects of subconscious vibrations within you or they are vibratory causes of the corresponding vibrations within you. A disciplined man never permits them to be causes unless they awaken in him the desirable states of consciousness. With a knowledge of the law of reversibility, the disciplined man transforms his world by imagining and feeling only what is lovely and of good report. The beautiful idea he awakens within himself shall not fail to arouse its affinity in others. He knows the savior of the world is not a man but the manifestation that would save. The sick man's savior is health, the hungry man's is food, the thirsty man's savior is water. He walks in the company of the savior by assuming the feeling of his wish fulfilled. By the law of reversibility, that all transformations of force are reversible, the energy or feeling awakened transforms itself into the state imagined. He never waits four months for the harvest. If in four months the harvest will awaken in him a state of joy, then, inversely, the joy of harvest now will awaken the harvest now. "Now is the acceptable time to give beauty for ashes, joy for mourning, praise for the spirit of heaviness; that they might be called trees of righteousness, the planting of the Lord that he might be glorified."

CHAPTER 4

Energy and Power

Everyone is amenable to the same psychological laws which govern the ordinary hypnotic subject. He is amenable to control by suggestion. In hypnosis, the objective senses are partly or totally suspended. However, no matter how profoundly the objective senses are locked in hypnosis, the subjective faculties are alert, and the subject recognizes everything that goes on around him. The activity and power of the subjective mind are proportionate to the sleep of the objective mind. Suggestions which appear powerless when presented directly to the objective consciousness are highly efficacious when the subject is in a hypnotic state. The hypnotic state is simply being unaware, objectively. In hypnotism, the conscious mind is put to sleep and the subconscious powers are exposed as to be directly reached by suggestion. It is easy to see from this, providing you accept the truth of mental suggestions, that anyone not objectively aware of you is in a profound hypnotic state relative to you. Therefore "Curse not the king, no not in thy thought; and curse not the rich in the bedchamber; for a bird of the air shall carry the voice, and that which hath wings shall tell the matter" (Ecc. 10:20). What you sincerely believe as true of another you will awaken within him.

No one need be entranced, in the ordinary manner, to be helped. If the subject is consciously unaware of the suggestion, and if the suggestion is given with conviction and confidently accepted by the operator as true, then you have the ideal setting for a successful prayer. Represent the subject to yourself mentally as though he had already done that which you desire him to do. Mentally speak to him and congratulate him on having done what you want him to do. Mentally see him in the state you want him to obtain. Within the circle of its action, every word subjectively spoken awakens objectively, what it affirms. Incredulity on the part of the subject is no hindrance when you are in control of your reverie.

Bold assertion by you, while you are in a partly subjective state, awakens what you affirm. Self-confidence on your part and the thorough belief in the truth of your mental assertion are all that is needed to produce results. Visualize the subject and imagine that you hear his voice. This establishes contact with his subjective mind. Then imagine that he is telling you what you want to hear. If you want to send him words of health and wealth, then imagine that he is telling you "I have never felt better and I have never had more," and mentally tell him of your joy in witnessing his good fortune. Imagine that you see and hear his joy.

A mental conversation with the subjective image of another must be in a manner which does not express the slightest doubt as to the truth of what you hear and say. If you have the least idea that you do not believe what you have imagined you have heard and seen, the subject will not comply, for your subjective mind will transmit only your fixed ideas. Only fixed ideas can awaken their vibratory correlates in those toward whom they are directed. In the controlled reverie, ideas must be suggested with the utmost care. If you do not control your imagination in the reverie, your imagination will control you. Whatever you suggest with confidence is law to the subjective mind; it is under obligation to objectify that which you mentally affirm. Not only does the subject execute the state affirmed but he does it as though the decision had come of itself, or the idea or the idea had originated by him.

Control of the subconscious is dominion over everything. Each state obeys one mind's control. Control of the subconscious is accomplished through control of your beliefs, which in turn is the all-potent factor in the visible states. Imagination and faith are the secrets of creation.

CHAPTER 5

Law of thought Transmission

"He sent his word and healed them and delivered them from their destructions." He transmitted the consciousness of health and awoke its vibratory correlate in the one toward whom it was directed. He mentally represented the subject to himself in a state of health and imagined he heard the subject confirm it. "For no word of God shall be void of power; therefore, hold fast the pattern of healthful words which thou has heard."

To pray successfully you must have clearly defined objectives. You must know what you want before you can ask for it. You must know what you want before you can feel that you have it, and prayer is the feeling of the fulfilled desire. It does not matter what it is you seek in prayer, or where it is, or whom it concerns. You have nothing to do but convince yourself of the truth of that which you desire to see manifested. When you emerge from prayer you no longer seek, for you have—if you have prayed correctly—subconsciously assumed the reality of the state sought, and by the law of reversibility your subconscious must objectify that which it affirms.

You must have a conductor to transmit a force. You may employ a wire, a jet of water, a current of air, a ray of light or any intermediary whatsoever. The principle of the photophone or the transmission of the voice by light will help you to understand thought transmission, or the sending of a word to heal another. There is a strong analogy between a spoken voice and a mental voice. To think is to speak low, to speak is to think aloud. The principle of the photophone is this: A ray of light is reflected by a mirror and projected to a receiver at a distant point. Back of the mirror is a mouthpiece. By speaking into the mouthpiece you cause the mirror to vibrate. A vibrating mirror modifies the light reflected on it. The modified light has your speech to carry, not as speech, but as represented in its mechanical correlate. It reaches the distant station and impinges on a disc within the receiver; it causes the disc to vibrate according to the modification it undergoes—and it reproduces your voice.

"I am the light of the world." I am, the knowledge that I exist, is a light by means of which what passes in my mind is rendered visible. Memory, or my ability to mentally see what is objectively present, proves that my mind is a mirror, so sensitive a mirror that it can reflect a thought. The re-perception of an image in memory in no way differs as a visual act from the perception of my image in a mirror. The same principle of seeing is involved in both.

Your consciousness is the light reflected on the mirror of your mind and projected in space to the one of whom you think. By mentally speaking to the subjective image in your mind you cause the mirror of your mind to vibrate. Your vibrating mind modifies the light of consciousness reflected on it. The modified light of consciousness reaches the one toward whom it is directed and impinges on the mirror of his mind; it causes his mind to vibrate according to the modification it undergoes. Thus, it reproduces in him what was mentally affirmed by you.

Your beliefs, your fixed attitudes of mind, constantly modify your consciousness as it is reflected on the mirror of your mind. Your consciousness, modified by your beliefs, objectifies itself in the conditions of your world. To change your world, you must first change your conception of it. To change a man, you must change your conception of him. You must first believe him to be the man you want him to be and mentally talk to him as though he were. All men are sufficiently sensitive to reproduce your beliefs of them. Therefore, if your word is not reproduced visibly in him toward whom it is sent, the cause is to be found in you, not in the subject.

As soon as you believe in the truth of the state affirmed, results follow. Everyone can be transformed; every thought can be transmitted; every thought can be visibly embodied.

Subjective words - subconscious assumptions - awaken what they affirm. "They are living and active and shall not return unto me void, but shall accomplish that which I please, and shall prosper in the thing whereto I sent them." They are endowed with the intelligence pertaining to their mission and will persist until the object of their existence is realized; they persist until they awaken the vibratory correlates of themselves within the one toward whom they are directed, but the moment the object of their creation is accomplished they cease to be. The word spoken subjectively in quiet confidence will always awaken a corresponding state in the one in whom it was spoken; but the moment its task is accomplished it ceases to be, permitting the one in whom the state is realized to remain in the consciousness of the state affirmed or to return to his former state.

Whatever state has your attention holds your life. Therefore, to become attentive to a former state is to return to that condition. "Remember not the former things, neither consider things of old."

Nothing can be added to man, for the whole of creation is already perfected in him. "The kingdom of heaven is within you." "Man can receive nothing, except it be given him from heaven." Heaven is your subconsciousness. Not even a sunburn is given from without. The rays without only awaken corresponding rays within. Were the burning rays not contained within man, all the concentrated rays in the universe could not burn him. Were the tones of health not contained within the consciousness of the one whom they are affirmed, they could not be vibrated by the word which is sent. You do not really give to another—you resurrect that which is asleep within him. "The damsel is not dead, but sleepeth." Death is merely a sleeping and forgetting. Age and decay are the sleep—not death—of youth and health. Recognition of a state vibrates or awakens it.

Distance, as it is cognized by your objective senses, does not exist for the subjective mind. "If I take the wings of the morning, and dwell in the uttermost parts of the sea; even there shall they hand lead me." Time and space are conditions of thought; the imagination can transcend them and move in a psychological time and space. Although physically separated from a place by thousands of miles, you can mentally live in the distant place as though it were here. Your imagination can easily transform winter into summer, New York into Florida, and so on. Whether the object of your desire be near or far, results will be the same. Subjectively, the object of your desire is never far off; its intense nearness makes it remote from observation of the senses. It dwells in consciousness, and consciousness is closer than breathing and nearer than hands and feet.

Consciousness is the one and only reality. All phenomena are formed of the same substance vibrating at different rates. Out of consciousness I as man came, and to consciousness I as man return. In consciousness all states exist subjectively and are awakened to their objective existence by belief. The only thing that prevents us from making a successful subjective impression on one at a great distance, or transforming there into here, is our habit of regarding space as an obstacle.

A friend a thousand miles away is rooted in your consciousness through your fixed ideas of him. To think of him and represent him to yourself inwardly in the state you desire him to be, confident that this subjective image is as true as it were already objectified, awakens in him a corresponding state which he must objectify. The results will be as obvious as the cause was hidden. The subject will express the awakened state within him and remain unaware of the true cause of his action. Your illusion of free will is but ignorance of the causes which make you act. Prayers depend upon your attitude of mind for their success and not upon the attitude of the subject. The subject has no power to resist your controlled subjective ideas of him unless the state affirmed by you to be true of him is a state he is incapable of wishing as true of another. In that case it returns to you, the sender, and will realize itself in you. Provided the idea is acceptable, success depends entirely on the operator not upon the subject who, like compass needles on their pivots, are quite indifferent as to what direction you choose to give them. If your fixed idea is not subjectively accepted by the one toward whom it is directed, it rebounds to you from whom it came. "Who is he that will harm you, if ye be followers of that which is good? I have been young, and now am old; yet have I not seen the righteous forsaken, nor his seed begging bread." "There shall no evil happen to the just." Nothing befalls us that is not of the nature of ourselves.

A person who directs a malicious thought to another will be injured by its rebound if he fails to get subconscious acceptance of the other. "As ye sow, so shall ye reap." Furthermore, what you can wish and believe of another can be wished and believed of you, and you have no power to reject it if the one who desires it for you accepts it as true of you. The only power to reject a subjective word is to be incapable of wishing a similar state of another—to give presupposes the ability to receive. The possibility to impress an idea upon another mind presupposes the ability of that mind to receive that impression. Fools exploit the world; the wise transfigure it. It is the highest wisdom to know that in the living universe there is no destiny other than that created out of imagination of man. There is no influence outside of the mind of man.

"Whatsoever things are lovely, whatsoever are of good report; if there be any virtue and if there be any praise, think on these things." Never accept as true of others what you would not want to be true of you. To awaken a state within another it must first be awake within you. The state you would transmit to another can only be transmitted if it is believed by you. Therefore, to give is to receive. You cannot give what you do not have, and you have only what you believe. So, to believe a state as true of another not only awakens that state within the other but it makes it alive within you. You are what you believe.

"Give and ye shall receive, full measure, pressed down and running over." Giving is simply believing, for what you truly believe of others you will awaken within them. The vibratory state transmitted by your belief persists until it awakens its corresponding vibration in him of whom it is believed. But before it can be transmitted it must first be awake within the transmitter. Whatever is awake within your consciousness, you are.

Whether the belief pertains to self or another does not matter, for the believer is defined by the sum total of his beliefs or subconscious assumptions.

"As a man thinketh in his heart"—in the deep subconscious of himself—"so is he." Disregard appearances and subjectively affirm as true that which you wish to be true. This awakens in you the tone of the state affirmed which in turn realizes itself in you and in the one of whom it is affirmed. Give and ye shall receive. Beliefs invariably awaken what they affirm. The world is a mirror wherein everyone sees himself reflected. The objective world reflects the beliefs of the subjective mind.

Some people are self-impressed best by visual images, others by mental sounds, and still others by mental actions. The form of mental activity which allows the whole power of your attention to be focused in one chosen direction is the one to cultivate, until you can bring all to play on your objective at the same time.

Should you have difficulty in understanding the terms, "visual images," "mental sounds" and "mental actions," here is an illustration that should make their meanings clear: A imagines he sees a piece of music, knowing nothing at all about musical notations. The impression in his mind is purely *visual image*. B imagines he sees the same piece, but he can read music and can imagine how it would sound when played on the piano; that imagination is *mental sound*. C also reads music and is a pianist; as he reads, he imagines himself playing the piece. The imaginary action is *mental action*.

The visual images, mental sounds and mental actions are creations of your imagination, and though they appear to come from without, they actually come from within yourself. They move as if moved by another but are really launched by your own spirit from the magical store-house of imagination. They are projected into space by the same vibratory law that governs the sending of a voice or picture. Speech and images are projected not as speech or images but as vibratory correlates. Subjective mind vibrates according to the modifications it undergoes by the thought and feelings of the operator. The visible state created is the effect of the subjective vibrations. A feeling is always accompanied by a corresponding vibration, that is, a change in expression or sensation in the operator.

There is no thought or feeling without expression. No matter how emotionless you appear to be if you reflect with any degree of intensity, there is always an execution of slight muscular movements. The eye, though shut, follows the movements of the imaginary objects and the pupil is dilated or contracted according to the brightness or the remoteness of those objects; respiration is accelerated or slowed, according to the course of your thoughts; the muscles contract correspondingly to your mental movements.

This change of vibration persists until it awakens a corresponding vibration in the subject, which vibration then expresses itself in a physical fact. "And the word was made flesh." Energy, as you see in the case of radio, is transmitted and received in a "field," a place where changes in space occur. The field and energy are one and inseparable. The field or subject becomes the embodiment of the word or energy received. The thinker and the thought, the operator and the subject, the energy and the field are one. Were you still enough to hear the sound of your beliefs you would know what is meant by "the music of the spheres." The mental sound you hear in prayer as coming from without is really produced by yourself. Self-observation will reveal this fact. As the music of the spheres is defined as the harmony heard by the gods alone and is supposed to be produced by the movements of the celestial spheres , so, too, is the harmony you subjectively hear for others heard by you alone is produced by the movements of your thoughts and feelings in the true kingdom or "heaven within you."

CHAPTER 6

Good Tidings

"How beautiful upon the mountains are the feet of him that bringeth good tidings, that publisheth peace, that bringeth good tidings of good, that pubisheth salvation."

A very effective way to bring good tidings to another is to call before your minds eyes the subjective image of the person you wish to help and have him affirm that which you desired him to do. Mentally hear him tell you he has done it. This awakens within him the vibratory correlate of the state affirmed, which vibration persists until its mission is accomplished. It does not matter what it is you desire to have done, or whom you select to do it. As soon as you subjectively affirm that it is done, results follow. Failure can result only if you fail to accept the truth of your assertion or if the state affirmed would not be desired by the subject for himself or another. In the latter event, the state would realize itself in you, the operator.

The seemingly harmless habit of "talking to yourself" is the most fruitful form of prayer. A mental argument with the subjective image of another is the surest way to pray for an argument. You are asking to be offended by the other when you objectively meet. He is compelled to act in a manner displeasing to you, unless before the meeting you countermand or modify your order by subjectively affirming a change.

Unfortunately, man forgets his subjective arguments, his daily mental conversations with others, and so is at a loss for an explanation of the conflicts and misfortunes of his life. As mental arguments produce conflicts, so happy mental conversations produce corresponding visible states of good tidings. Man creates himself out of his own imagination.

If the state desired is for yourself and you find it difficult to accept as true what your senses deny, call before your mind's eye the subjective image of a friend and have him mentally affirm that you are already that which you desire to be. This establishes in him, without his conscious consent or knowledge, the subconscious assumption that you are that which he mentally affirmed, which assumption, because it is unconsciously assumed, will persist until it fulfills its mission. Its mission is to awaken in your its vibratory correlate, which vibration when awakened in you realizes itself as an objective fact.

Another very effective way to pray for oneself is to use the formula of Job who found that his own captivity was removed as he prayed for his friends. Fix your attention on a friend and have the imaginary voice of your friend tell you that he is, or has, that which is comparable to that which you desire to be or have. As you mentally hear and see him, feel the thrill of his good fortune and sincerely wish him well. This awakens in him the corresponding vibration of the state affirmed, which vibration must then objectify itself as a physical fact. You will discover the truth of the statement, "Blessed are the merciful for they shall receive mercy." "The quality of mercy is twice blessed—it blesses him who taketh and him who giveth." The good you subjectively accept as true of others will not only be expressed by them, but a full share will be realized by you.

Transformations are never total. Force A is always transformed into more than a force B. A blow with a hammer produces not only a mechanical concussion, but also heat, electricity, a sound, a magnetic change and so on. The vibratory correlate in the subject is not the entire transformation of the sentiment communicated. The gift transmitted to another is the like the divine measure, pressed down, shaken together and running over, so that after five thousand are fed from the five loaves and two fish, twelve baskets full are left over.

CHAPTER 7

The Greatest Prayer

Imagination is the beginning of creation. You imagine what you desire, and then you believe it to be true. Every dream could be realized by those self-disciplined enough to believe it. People are what you choose to make them; a man is according to the manner in which you look at him. You must look at him with different eyes before he will objectively change. "Two men looked from prison bars, one saw the mud and the other saw the stars." Centuries ago, Isaiah asked the question; "Who is blind, but my servant, or deaf, as my messenger that I sent?" "Who is blind as he that is perfect, as blind as the Lord's servant?" The perfect man judges not after appearances, but judges righteously. He sees others as he desires them to be;

he hears only what he wants to hear. He sees only good in others. In him is no condemnation for the transforms the world with his seeing and hearing.

"The king that sitteth on the throne scattereth the evil with his eye." Sympathy for living things—agreement with human limitations—is not in the consciousness of the king because he has learned to separate their false concepts from their true being. To him poverty is but the sleep of wealth. He does not see caterpillars, but painted butterflies to be; not winter, but summer sleeping; not man in want, but Jesus sleeping. Jesus of Nazareth, who scattered the evil with his eye, is asleep in the imagination of every man, and out of his own imagination must man awaken him by subjectively affirming "I AM Jesus" Then and only then will he see Jesus, for man can only see what is awake in himself. The holy womb is man's imagination. The holy child is that conception of himself which fits Isaiah's definition of perfection. Heed the words of St. Augustine, "Too late have

I loved thee, for behold thou were within and it was without that I did seek thee." It is your own consciousness that you must turn as to the only reality. There, and there alone, you awaken that which is asleep. "Though Christ a thousand times in Bethlehem be born, if He is not born of in thee thy soul is still forlorn."

Creation is finished. You call your creation into being by feeling the reality of the state you would call. A mood attracts its affinities, but it does not create what it attracts. As sleep is called by feeling "I am sleepy," so, too, is Jesus Christ called by the feeling, "I am Jesus Christ." Man sees only himself. Nothing befalls man that is not the nature of himself. People emerge out of the mass betraying their close affinity to your moods as they are engendered. You meet them seemingly by accident but find they are intimates of your moods. Because your moods continually externalize themselves you could prophesy from your moods, that you, without search, would soon meet certain characters and encounter certain conditions.

Therefore, call the perfect one into being by living in the feeling, "I am Christ," for Christ is the one concept of self through which can be seen the unveiled realities of eternity.

Our behavior is influenced by our subconscious assumption respecting our own social and intellectual rank and that of the one we are addressing. Let us seek for and evoke the greatest rank, and the noblest of all is that which disrobes man of his morality and clothes him with uncurbed immortal glory. Let us assume the feeling "I am Christ," and our whole behavior will subtly and unconsciously change in accordance with the assumption.

Our subconscious assumptions continually externalize themselves that others may consciously see us as we subconsciously see ourselves and tell us by their actions what we have subconsciously assumed of ourselves to be. Therefore, let us assume the feeling "I AM Christ," until our conscious claim becomes our subconscious assumption that

"We all with open face beholding as in a glass the glory of the Lord are changed into the same image from *glory to glory.*" *Let God Awake and his enemies be destroyed. There is no greater prayer for man.*

OTHER BOOKS YOU MAY LIKE

- 1984 by George Orwell, ISBN: 9789380914947
- 12 Years a Slave by Solomon Northup, ISBN: 9789390492374
- A Passage to India by E.M. Forster, ISBN: 9789354990205
- A Room of One's Own by Virginia Woolf, ISBN: 9789354990281
- A Streetcar Named Desire by Tennessee Williams, ISBN: 9788194748601
- A Wrinkle in Time by Madeleine L'Engle, ISBN: 9789354991066
- Abraham Lincoln by Lord Charnwood, ISBN: 9789380914251
- Animal Farm by George Orwell, ISBN: 9789380914701
- Annihilation of Caste by Dr B.R. Ambedkar, ISBN: 9789390492732
- Anthem by Ayn Rand, ISBN: 9789389157079
- As a Man Thinketh by James Allen, ISBN: 9788180320262
- As I Lay Dying by William Faulkner, ISBN: 9789390492381
- Believe in Yourself by Joseph Murphy, ISBN: 9789388118385
- Chanakya Neeti by Chanakya, ISBN: 9789389716276
- Civilization and Its Discontents by Sigmund Freud, ISBN: 9789387669499
- Demian by Hermann Hesse, ISBN: 9789387669567
- George Orwell Combo : Animal Farm & 1984, ISBN: 9789390492459
- Gravity by George Gamow, ISBN: 9789388118484
- Guerrilla Warfare by Ernesto Che Guevara, ISBN: 9789354990366
- How I Made $2,000,000 in the Stock Market by N. Darvas, ISBN: 9789389716283
- How to Attract Money by Joseph Murphy, ISBN: 9789388118408
- How to Develop Self Confidence by Dale Carnegie, ISBN: 9789387669000
- How to Enjoy Your Life and Your Job by Dale Carnegie, ISBN: 9789387669017
- How to Stop Worrying and Start Living by Dale Carnegie, ISBN: 9789380914817
- How to Win Friends and Influence People by D. Carnegie, ISBN: 9788180320217
- Jail Diary and Other Writings by Bhagat Singh, ISBN: 9789390492398

OTHER BOOKS YOU MAY LIKE

- Know Your Worth by NK Sondhi & Vibha Malhotra, ISBN: 9788180320231
- Lost Horizon by James Hilton, ISBN: 9789389716313
- Maneaters of Kumaon by Jim Corbett, ISBN: 9789354990731
- Mansarover 1 (Hindi) by Premchand, ISBN: 9789380914978
- Mansarover 2 (Hindi) by Premchand, ISBN: 9789380914985
- Meditation and Its Methods by Swami Vivekananda, ISBN: 9789389716320
- Meditations by Marcus Aurelius, ISBN: 9789388118736
- My Experiments with Truth by Mahatma Gandhi, ISBN: 9789387669291
- My Inventions: The Autobiography of Nikola Tesla, ISBN: 9789388118132
- One, None and a Hundred Thousand by Luigi Pirandello, ISBN: 9789389716337
- Relativity by Albert Einstein, ISBN: 9789380914220
- Reminiscences of a Stock Operator by Edwin Lefevre, ISBN: 9788194764816
- Scientific Healing Affirmations by P. Yogananda, ISBN: 9789389716344
- Selected Stories of Rabindranath Tagore by Tagore, ISBN: 9789380914770
- Siddhartha by Hermann Hesse, ISBN: 9789380914145
- Student's Encyclopedia of G.K. by GP Editors, ISBN: 9789380914190
- Success Through a Positive Mental Attitude by N. Hill, ISBN: 9789390492435
- Tales from Shakespeare by Charles Lamb & Mary Lamb, ISBN: 9789380914367
- The Art of War by Sun Tzu, ISBN: 9789380914893
- The Autobiography of a Yogi by Paramahansa Yogananda, ISBN: 9789380914602
- The Book of Enoch by Enoch, ISBN: 9789390492480
- The Diary of a Young Girl by Anne Frank, ISBN: 9789380914312
- The Dynamic Laws of Prosperity by Catherine Ponder, ISBN: 9789388118156
- The Elements of Style by William Strunk, ISBN: 9789389157123
- The Game of Life and How to Play It by Florence Shinn, ISBN: 9789387669390
- The Law of Success by Napoleon Hill, ISBN: 9788180320927

Develop your reading habit | **Gift books to your friends**

OTHER BOOKS YOU MAY LIKE

- The Light of Asia by Sir Edwin Arnold, ISBN: 9789380914923
- The Mysterious Affair at Styles by Agatha Christie, ISBN: 9789390492510
- The Origin of Species by Charles Darwin, ISBN: 9788180320453
- The Plague by Albert Camus, ISBN: 9788194764892
- The Power of Positive Thinking by Norman Vincent Peale, ISBN: 9789388118569
- The Power of Your Subconscious Mind by Joseph Murphy, ISBN: 9788180320958
- The Problem of Increasing Human Energy by Nikola Tesla, ISBN: 9789354990953
- The Prophet by Kahlil Gibran, ISBN: 9789380914022
- The Psychopathology of Everyday Life by Sigmund Freud, ISBN: 9789388118071
- The Railway Children by E Nesbit, ISBN: 9789354990960
- The Red Badge of Courage by Stephen Crane, ISBN: 9789354990977
- The Richest Man in Babylon by George S. Clason, ISBN: 9789387669369
- The Science of Getting Rich by Wallace D. Wattles, ISBN: 9788180320972
- The Sound and the Fury by William Faulkner, ISBN: 9789390492572
- The Stranger by Albert Camus, ISBN: 9789390492589
- The Sun Also Rises by Ernest Hemingway, ISBN: 9789354990984
- The World as I See It by Albert Einstein, ISBN: 9789388118125
- The Yoga Sutras of Patanjali by Patanjali, ISBN: 9789389716351
- Their Eyes Were Watching God by Zora Neale Hurston, ISBN: 9788194764885
- Think and Grow Rich by Napoleon Hill, ISBN: 9788180320255
- Thought Vibration by William Walker Atkinson, ISBN: 9789389157154
- To the Lighthouse by Virginia Woolf, ISBN: 9789390492190
- Who were the Shudras by Dr B.R. Ambedkar, ISBN: 9789354991028
- World's Best Short Stories: Volume 1 by Various Authors, ISBN: 9789390492275
- Wuthering Heights by Emily Brontë, ISBN: 9788193545898
- Zen in the Art of Archery by Eugen Herrigel, ISBN: 9789354991059

Develop your reading habit | **Gift books to your friends**

www.ingramcontent.com/pod-product-compliance
Ingram Content Group UK Ltd.
Pitfield, Milton Keynes, MK11 3LW, UK
UKHW040229300826
14791UKWH00001B/66

9 789354 994487